## A LIFE IN THE DARK

If they had called to her a few weeks earlier, Helen would have climbed out of bed and run, laughing, into her parents' arms. But Helen had been very sick. For days, the doctor had thought she might die. Now, finally, the fever was gone. Helen would live. But the Kellers were finding horrible changes in their only child.

Helen had been a perfectly healthy baby for a year and a half.

Now she could not see.

# Helen Keller

## A Light for the Blind

# KATHLEEN V. KUDLINSKI
## illustrated by Donna Diamond

PUFFIN BOOKS
An Imprint of Penguin Group (USA)

PUFFIN BOOKS
Published by the Penguin Group
Penguin Group (USA) LLC
375 Hudson Street
New York, New York 10014

USA * Canada * UK * Ireland * Australia
New Zealand * India * South Africa * China

penguin.com
A Penguin Random House Company

First published in the United States of America by Viking Penguin,
a division of Penguin Books USA Inc., 1989
Published by Puffin Books, 1991
Reissued by Puffin Books, an imprint of Penguin Young Readers Group, 2014

THE LIBRARY OF CONGRESS HAS CATALOGED THE PUFFIN EDITION AS FOLLOWS:
Kudlinski, Kathleen V.
Helen Keller : a light for the blind / by Kathleen V. Kudlinski ; illustrated by Donna Diamond.
p. cm.—(Women of our time)
ISBN 978-0-670-82460-1 (hardcover)
Summary: A biography detailing Helen Keller's adventurous life as she worked tirelessly
to lead the way for handicapped people.
[1. Keller, Helen, 1880–1968—Juvenile literature. 2. Keller, Helen, 1880-1968.
3. Deafblind women—United States—Biography—Juvenile literature. 4. Blind. 5. Deaf.
6. People with disabilities. 7. Women—biography.]
I. Diamond, Donna. II. Title.
HV1624.K4 K83 1989
89033914

Puffin Books ISBN 978-0-14-751467-7

Printed in the United States of America

1 3 5 7 9 10 8 6 4 2

*For Jane Yolen, M-e-n-t-o-r*

# CONTENTS

# one

Helen," Mrs. Keller called gently. Little Helen Keller went on playing in her crib. "Helen!" Mrs. Keller called again, louder. The pretty blond child did nothing. Mrs. Keller came right up behind Helen, put her lips next to her daughter's ear, and yelled, "Helen!" Her baby still didn't move.

Captain Keller brought a kerosene lantern into his child's room. He waved it about in front of her. Helen's bright blue eyes did not move. He held it right in front of her face and turned the flame up as bright as it could go. Though both he and his wife were squinting with the light, Helen stared right at it—without blinking.

If they had called to her a few weeks earlier, Helen would have climbed out of bed and run, laughing, into their arms. But Helen had been very sick. For days, the doctor had thought she might die. Now, finally, the fever was gone. Helen would live. But the Kellers were finding horrible changes in their only child.

Helen had been a perfectly healthy baby for a year and a half. Now she could not see. She could not hear, either. Captain and Mrs. Keller cried for their poor daughter. They told themselves that Helen might get over her blindness and deafness. Her eyes and ears might slowly heal. But Helen never did get better. That fever began what Helen later called "my long night." She lived the rest of her life in darkness and silence.

At first, Helen just lay crying unless her

mother was holding her. Soon she was following her mother around by holding onto her long skirts. Then she began to feel her way about their home in Tuscumbia, Alabama. It was hard to get lost in the tiny house. Captain Keller had built it almost as a playhouse after he came back from fighting in the Civil War. He had brought his new wife there, and there on June 27, 1880, Helen was born. It had only two rooms. The Kellers lived in one. The other was for a servant who kept the fires lit that chilly winter of 1881.

The rest of the servants and the Captain's two teenaged boys lived in the big main house a few steps away. The boys' mother had died years earlier. Kate, the Captain's new wife, was young and pretty. Helen went everywhere with her, her busy hands feeling everything her mother did.

Sometimes Helen's quick mind caught the meaning of what she could feel. Mrs. Keller wore fancy dresses only to go out, so Helen learned that when she felt lace and ruffles, her mother was about to leave. If someone handed her a nightgown, Helen knew it was time for bed, though day and night looked the same to her. When she felt the floorboards bounce a little, she knew someone was walking nearby.

Other things that Helen felt made no sense at all to her. She often felt piles of paper around her father. Sometimes Captain Keller would hold these papers in front of his face. Helen couldn't guess that he was reading, or that he owned the newspaper company that printed those papers. When her mother's mouth moved, Helen had no idea that she was talking.

There was no way Helen could learn to speak. She couldn't hear herself or anyone else talk. She soon forgot the few words she had learned as a baby. Without words, she couldn't ask when Mommy would come home. She couldn't say that her tummy hurt. She couldn't

say she was sorry. And she couldn't ask questions.

She made up other ways to get things that she wanted. To ask for bread, she moved her hands as if she were cutting a slice and spreading butter onto it. She nodded her head to say *yes*, pulled with her hands to mean *come*, and pushed for *go*. When she moved her mouth to make the sound "wa-wa" people gave her a drink of water. But the sign she came to use most was a shake of the head for *no*.

She wouldn't let anyone comb her curly blond hair, so it often hung in tangles. She wouldn't wash her face. She wouldn't sit in her chair at dinner and wait to be given food. Instead, she went from person to person, asking for food by moving her hands to her mouth and pretending to swallow.

While she was two and three years old, Helen was so cute that it didn't matter how she behaved. Everyone felt so sorry for her that she was never scolded. When her big blue eyes filled with tears, Captain Keller would let her have anything she wanted. Helen was becoming spoiled.

There were other reasons she was starting to act so badly. In the early years, all of Helen's time was spent learning how to move safely, how to eat, how to keep from being hurt, and how to stay near her mother and father. Like any other child, Helen wanted to do more things as she got older. But, unlike other children, she had no way to talk about her new thoughts and needs. She didn't know the words for them. She didn't even know what words were.

Having needs that weren't filled and problems that she couldn't solve made Helen cranky. Now, instead of feeling her way carefully around the house, she just stamped about. She pushed things out of her way—even things like glass lamps and vases of flowers! Now she went from place to place at the dinner table, grabbing handfuls of food from anyone's plate. She pinched people she didn't like and kicked and screamed when she didn't get her way. She remembered later that she would run outdoors "to find comfort and to hide my hot face in the cool leaves and grass after each tantrum."

After one awful visit to her grandmother's, Captain and Mrs. Keller were told never to bring Helen there again. Her aunts and uncles thought the sickness had ruined her brain as well as her eyes and ears. Helen's parents had guessed that she was very smart, but there was no way they could prove it.

In a book by the famous writer Mark Twain, Mrs. Keller read about a woman named Laura Bridgman. Laura was deaf and blind like Helen, but she had been taught to speak with her hands. Every letter of the alphabet had a finger sign, and Laura used this manual alphabet to spell out her wishes. She could "hear" by feeling other people's hands while they spelled with finger signs. Was 4-year-old Helen smart enough to learn like Laura?

The Kellers took Helen to see Alexander

Graham Bell in Philadelphia. Mr. Bell was famous for making the first telephone, but he spent most of his time trying to help the deaf. Helen sat on his lap while the grown-ups talked. She quickly learned finger games he showed her. Mr. Bell told the Kellers that Helen would do fine at Perkins School for the Blind in Boston. Laura Bridgman had studied there.

The Kellers went home to think about it. They didn't want Helen living so far from Alabama. They wrote to Boston to ask if a teacher could come to work with Helen in her own home. There was plenty of room, for they had moved back into the big main house. They had to, for now 6-year-old Helen had a baby sister, Mildred. Mrs. Keller was busy with the new baby. She didn't have time to figure out what Helen wanted or to hug her whenever she was frightened or angry. To make her feel better, she gave Helen a new baby doll to hold while she rocked Mildred.

One day, when Helen went to put her doll

into the cradle, she found Mildred lying there. In a temper, Helen knocked over the cradle, throwing her baby sister to the floor. Mrs. Keller saved Mildred from being hurt, but now they all knew something had to be done about Helen.

On March 3, 1887, the teacher from Perkins, Annie Sullivan, walked up the steps of the Kellers' front porch. She was young and pretty. She did not look strong and she could not see well. The Kellers wondered how she could ever handle wild little Helen. She had to. Annie was their only hope to give Helen happiness.

She did, but first she made Helen's life— and everyone else's—miserable.

# two

T - E - A - C - H - E - R

When the stranger on the steps tried to give her a hug, Helen pushed her away. Who was this woman? Had she brought something to eat? Strangers often did. Helen made her sign for eating and reached her hand into the new lady's bag.

To Helen's surprise, her hand was pushed aside, and the stranger entered the house, leaving her behind. No one ever did that. Helen followed the vibrations of footsteps up the stairs to where the stranger was unpacking in a bedroom. So this lady would stay. Helen again tried to feel through the stranger's bags. Instead of food, the stranger handed Helen a doll.

It was months before Helen learned that this doll was a gift from the blind children at Perkins or that it had been dressed by Laura Bridgman herself. There were many other things she had to learn first. The stranger pulled Helen's hand free of the doll and tapped a pattern into her palm. *"D-o-l-l,"* she spelled. *"D-o-l-l,"* Helen spelled back, copying the movements. She had no idea what it meant.

They played until it was time for dinner. At the table, Helen tried to grab a handful of food from the new lady's plate. The stranger pushed her greasy hand away and forced Helen back to her own chair. Helen was hungry. She tried to steal food again. She was pushed away. She pinched the stranger, stamped her feet, and kicked the chair. Still she got no food.

Helen went around to her Daddy's place where she always got what she wanted. Her Daddy was gone! Helen raced from place to place, finding that everyone had left, upset by her tantrum and Annie's strictness. Only the stranger was left at the table. Now Annie made Helen sit again and eat with a spoon. Helen hated using spoons. She couldn't see where the food was to scoop it up or see whether the food slipped off the spoon before it got to her mouth. In a temper, she threw it across the room.

The stranger pressed another spoon into her hand. For hours they battled over that first meal. Every meal after that was a fight. Whenever she could, Helen found her parents. They hated to watch Annie and Helen fight—and they were always fighting. Captain Keller would hug his daughter and give her candy to make her happy again. Her mother would rock her until she stopped crying.

About a week later, Helen walked with her

Daddy and the stranger along a path to the little house. The furniture seemed familiar but it was all moved around. Helen played a while, then felt for her Daddy. He was gone, but the lady was still there. Helen felt for the door. It was locked! The Kellers had agreed to let Annie work with Helen away from the family for a while.

Alone with the stranger, Helen was both scared and angry. They fought about eating, about dressing, about bedtimes and about washing. Helen punched and kicked, bit and pinched. She even broke two of the stranger's teeth. But still the lady made her do things the right way.

Annie did have interesting games to play. There were beads of different shapes and sizes to string in pretty patterns. The lady showed her many more finger games. Helen learned to move her fingers to make the sign for every letter of the alphabet, though she still had no idea what letters were. She memorized the patterns of many word spellings, and even tried to teach the manual alphabet to her dog, Belle. It made as much sense to the dog as it did to Helen, but it was fun.

When Helen did what the lady wanted, and did it with a smile, she was rewarded with a warm pat on the shoulder. Helen would do almost anything to get those pats, but she still wouldn't let the stranger hug her.

It was a different Helen who moved back to the main house with the stranger a week later. She still had a temper, but she had learned that tantrums no longer worked. She still ran to her father when she was very angry, but she was beginning to trust this stranger. It was nice to have someone pay attention to her all day long. The stranger was always fair and she had so many new games to teach.

One morning, one month and two days after the stranger had first come to Alabama, she taught Helen something that changed her life forever. They had been playing the finger games and holding a mug, the new doll, and some water. It made no sense to Helen and she grew tired, then cross. Suddenly she smashed her doll to the floor. The stranger swept up the pieces and led Helen outside.

Together they walked to the pump. As the stranger worked the handle, Helen reached her hands into the fresh water. Suddenly the stranger's hands met hers in the cold stream, and made one of the finger patterns they had been practicing. Helen repeated it, and began to tremble. "I knew then," Helen later wrote, "that *w-a-t-e-r* meant the wonderful cool something that was flowing over my hand. That living word awakened my soul, gave it light, hope, joy, set it free!"

Finally here was a way to let others know what she was thinking—and to learn what they thought as well. "It was as if I had come back to life after being dead." Helen remembered. "Sweet strange things that were locked up in my heart began to sing."

Helen pointed toward the stranger and held out her hand to ask, "Who are you?" *T-e-a-c-h-e-r*, the lady signed into Helen's damp hand. That was the name Helen called Annie for the rest of her life.

A nursemaid carried little Mildred by and Helen learned that this was *b-a-b-y*. The swinging wood was a *d-o-o-r*, that could *o-p-e-n* or *s-h-u-t*. By the end of the day, Helen had learned 30 words. That evening, for the first time, she gave Teacher a loving goodnight kiss.

Now Helen wanted to know the names of everything and how to use all of these exciting new words. Every word she added gave her a way to ask more questions. There was no stopping her mind—or her fingers. Helen's hands even "talked" in her sleep!

Teacher was kept busy every moment of the day, helping Helen make up for all those empty years of silence and darkness. She was a very strict teacher. Helen was not allowed to make any mistakes. Within months, Helen

was writing on a special tablet that had lines she could feel.

Then Annie began teaching her to read Braille (say "brale"). Every letter has a pattern of tiny paper bumps in Braille, bumps that Helen could feel. Each letter has to be the size of a fingertip, so this kind of writing takes up a lot of space. Helen could hardly lift the huge Braille books that the Perkins School sent to her. Annie made her practice everything until her work was perfect. It was hard learning with such a strict teacher, but Annie made it fun, too.

Together, they felt as tiny chicks pecked their way out of eggshells. They felt flower buds open into giant lilies. Annie showed Helen how to skip and taught her to giggle by tickling her in the warm Alabama sunshine. She read book after book into Helen's hand as they sat together on a branch in an old apple tree. Helen loved feeling the strong beat of poetry. The stories and poems showed her a world she had never even dreamed might exist.

Teacher led Helen around on her pony, Black Beauty, and taught her the names of the flowers she smelled along the way. Helen loved to ride. The rocking bounce of the saddle felt good. When she got off, she would pat Black Beauty's furry, warm sides and soft nose. She loved the "spicy, clovery smell of his breath."

When they visited a circus, Helen shook hands with a trained bear, patted a leopard, and felt the ears of a giraffe. She was angry for a moment when the soft, warm tip of an elephant's trunk stole a peanut from her hand. She stood very still as a great snake wrapped its coils around her, and she even put her fingers into the mouth of a tame lion.

News of Helen's adventures and her growth out of silence were so exciting that newspapers began to write about her. The head of Perkins School for the Blind, Mr. Anagnos, told everyone about the amazing child and the teacher who had come from his school. He printed the letters he got from both of them in Perkins's yearbooks. Soon people around the world

knew about Helen and her teacher. Helen had no idea she was famous.

She learned only what Annie wanted her to know. Annie made sure she read and heard the very best books, the finest poetry, and letters that the most important people had written to her. Things Helen had written herself were always corrected by Teacher. All of Helen's thoughts were shaped by Annie's hand as it spelled into her palm.

Helen couldn't read a comic book or see a newspaper or listen as people chatted with one another. She had no idea how other children thought or talked. She thought everyone else was just as good and kind as she tried to be. Her life was full of joy and gentleness. Just knowing how sweet Helen was made others feel wonderful.

Not knowing much about others was to hurt Helen badly.

# three

## THE TRUTH ABOUT HELEN

In 1888, Annie and Helen visited Perkins School for the Blind in Massachusetts. There, all the teachers and students spoke with the manual alphabet. "What a joy," Helen said later, "to talk with other children in my own language!" She met Laura Bridgman and thanked her for the doll. She missed her family and her dog. But she was learning even faster at Perkins with Annie and the other teachers to help her.

She spent the summer visiting with friends

at the seashore. Helen walked boldly into the water the first time she went to the beach. The first few waves rocked her gently. The next one tossed her under the water. She coughed and signed angrily, "Who put salt in water?!" Soon she was swimming through the waves, tied to the shore with a rope so she couldn't go out too far.

Then it was home for the fall and back to Perkins for the winter months. She spent the next few years this way, traveling between home and school and a growing number of friends' homes. Many people invited her to parties or asked to meet the famous little girl. There just wasn't time for everyone. Annie and Mr. Anagnos chose the rich and famous, like Mark Twain and Alexander Graham Bell, to meet her. Other people were told Helen was just too busy.

In 1889, Helen asked these special friends to help a 5-year-old boy who was deaf and blind like her. Unlike Helen, Tommy Stringer had no family or friends to send him to special schools. For the first time, 9-year-old Helen used her writing and her fame in the newspapers to help others. From around the world came money to have Tommy brought to the Perkins kindergarten.

When people heard that Helen's dog, Lioness, had died in Alabama, many of them sent her money for a new dog. She saved it all for Tommy. Finally there was enough to hire a special teacher for him, too. It seemed to Helen that if she were good and kind, she could do anything.

The next year, she decided to learn to talk out loud. Annie had always worried about how Helen would look to others. She made Helen walk gracefully, without feeling her way. She had to keep a pretty expression on her face and dress carefully. Annie had even tied Helen's hands behind her back for a whole day to teach her to stop biting her nails. Teacher did not want Helen to speak, worrying that her voice would be ugly. For the first time, Helen went against Annie's wishes.

Helen knew how to make sound. She could feel her own throat vibrate when she hummed, though she could not tell how high or how loud the noise was. She took some lessons in 1890, but learned the most by using Annie's mouth as a model. Annie would say a word while Helen felt her lips move. Then Helen would put her hand into Teacher's mouth while she talked to feel how her tongue and teeth should move. It made Annie's mouth ache, but slowly Helen learned to talk a little.

As Annie had feared, Helen never learned to speak clearly. For years, only her teacher and her family could understand anything she said. But once Helen could talk aloud, she stopped using hand signs. Annie had to explain to everyone what Helen was trying to say to them. Feeling Annie's mouth had shown Helen a new way to "hear." If she set her thumb lightly on a friend's throat, a finger across his lips

and another against his nose as he spoke, Helen could tell what he was saying.

Helen still enjoyed writing more than speaking. In 1892, she wrote a story called "The Frost King." After Annie made her correct the spelling and wording, Helen sent it to Mr. Anagnos as a birthday present. He loved the gentle story of frost fairies bringing color to the woodlands. The Perkins yearbook was just going to the printer, so Mr. Anagnos sent Helen's story, too. After it was printed, someone realized that it was not Helen's story at all! They said she had copied the story, stealing it from an old book by Margaret T. Canby.

Helen's story, "The Frost King," was almost exactly the same as Miss Canby's, "The Frost Fairies." She had even used many of the same words. Helen's amazing memory and sharp mind had helped her to be a top student. Now it had hurt her.

"The Frost Fairies" had been read into her hand three years before. She didn't even remember it. But when she smelled damp fall leaves and felt the first crisp frost, Miss Canby's ideas came back to her as if they were her own. Helen argued that she would never mean to steal words and ideas from another writer. But she had no proof. "I love the beautiful truth with my whole heart and mind," she said. Surely everyone would believe her.

Not everyone did. Perkins held a court to decide if she was lying. For two hours, they kept asking Helen if she had copied the story on purpose. They made Annie wait outside in the hall. Even when it was over, they weren't sure they believed Helen. That night she sobbed herself to sleep. "I felt so cold," she remembered later. "I imagined I should die before morning."

Helen's friends were angry at the way Perkins was treating her. The writer Mark Twain told the newspapers that every writer borrows ideas and adds to them as he writes. Miss Canby said it was an honor that Helen had remembered her story so clearly. But the damage was done.

The newspapers wondered if Helen was lying. Did she even know what the truth was? Perhaps Annie had tricked them all along about how smart Helen was. They even wondered if Mr. Anagnos had made up the whole story about Helen and Annie to get money and fame for the Perkins School.

All of this hurt. After that school year, Helen never went back to Perkins. They hadn't believed her there. She had trouble writing anything, for now she didn't even know whether to believe herself. What if she were just remembering something else from years ago? What if she really wasn't smart after all?

For a long while, she hurt inside. Then she got mad. She would show them! For proof that no one could question, Helen decided she would go to college. To get ready, Annie and Helen had to study for a few years at a school in New York City and another near Boston.

They chose schools that weren't specially for blind children, to prove that Helen was really doing the same work as any other student. That meant extra work for both of them. A few of the books were already printed in Braille. The tips of Helen's fingers sometimes bled from rubbing them across the bumpy Braille printing. Annie had to read other books in different languages for hours every day so she could spell them into Helen's hand. In each class, Annie went along to explain what the teachers were saying or writing on the blackboard.

Annie's eyes had always been weak, and now they were failing. To make it easier, Helen tried never to ask her to read anything a second time. Both of them worked until they were nearly ill, but Helen was proving something to herself and the world with every good grade she earned.

All this cost money. The Kellers couldn't afford it, so Helen asked her rich friends for loans. They were glad to promise money for

the rest of Helen's schooling. They were not so happy about lending Helen money to give to her father. Captain Keller had been taking money from her for years and asking her to try to get more. When he died in 1896, Helen missed him dreadfully. But it was a relief to have her friends in charge of her money.

Helen decided to go to Radcliffe, near Boston, because that school did not want her to study there. They didn't want to be bothered with a student who had special needs. When Helen passed the same tests that all other students had to take, the college had to say yes. Radcliffe did nothing to make it easier for Helen—and that was just the way she wanted it. College wasn't all work, though. Helen enjoyed dances and chess games with other students. She swam in a pool along a rope guideline and sledded down snowy hillsides with her friends. They gave her a Boston terrier because they knew how much she loved dogs.

While she was a student, the *Ladies' Home Journal* magazine asked her to write the story of her life for them. Soon Helen would have to be earning her own living. The magazine would pay her well for this story. It was a start. Helen still liked doing things for others, the way she had helped Tommy Stringer. Perhaps reading her article would help others who had problems, too.

The writing went well, but it was hard being a writer and a student at the same time. She needed help. A young man, John Macy, was hired to work as her editor. He put her writing in order and got it ready for the magazine. He was gentle and patient with her. Helen and Annie both liked him. After the articles were written, John helped to make them into a book.

*The Story of My Life* was published in 1903. It included Helen's story plus letters and reports Annie had written while Helen was growing up. The last part was written by John Macy.

With the money from the book, Helen bought a house in Wrentham, Massachusetts, near Boston. Mrs. Keller joined Annie and Helen to live there while Helen finished her college work. During her last year at Radcliffe, Helen wrote another, very short book, called *Optimism*. It explained how sure she was that things will always happen for the best. They always had for her.

At last it was graduation day, June 28, 1904. After many years, Helen was full of joy again. There could be no question now. At 23, she had written two books, bought her own house, and earned a college degree. She had proven the truth to herself and everyone else. A good and kind person—with or without handicaps—could do anything.

# four

ON HER OWN

John Macy often came to Helen and Teacher's house in Wrentham. He fixed a walking path for Helen with a rope fence that she could follow alone. He built extra bookcases for Helen's Braille books. He went with Helen and Annie to a giant national fair held in St. Louis in 1904.

That same week, a big meeting of teachers of the blind and the deaf was also held in St. Louis. The fair had a Helen Keller Day to honor Teacher and her famous student.

Crowds followed Helen wherever she went. They even took the flowers off her hat to help them remember their meeting with the wonderful woman. It showed Helen how much people cared about her, what she had done, and what she had to say.

Soon after they returned to Wrentham, John and Annie had something to say to Helen. They had decided to be married! Annie told her that she would never leave her side. John would move into the house with them. He could work there on his own books and poetry and still help Helen with her writing.

Helen was working on another book about herself, called *The World I Live In*. She would have liked to write about something else for a change. But her fans wanted to know still more about her life.

She was often asked how she could write about colors when she couldn't remember ever seeing them. Helen explained that when she said pink, she imagined rosebuds; green was young plants. She thought of red as warmth. Blue meant great open spaces to Helen and purple made her think of strong, deep feelings. Yellow stood for joy and sweet, warm sunlight.

"How can you tell if it is day or night?" was another common question. Helen said that the air felt lighter to her in the day. Smells were fainter, too. She could feel more breezes in the air and bouncing in the ground as people passed by with their horses and carriages.

Besides writing books and articles, Helen was making money by giving speeches. The groups of people who hired her listened quietly. Even so, Annie still had to repeat most of what Helen said. Her student's voice moved from loud to soft, from squeaky to deep, and from scratchy to slurred—often all in the same sentence. Helen's voice may have been awful, but her message was always joyful and cheerful.

In a magazine article, she wrote to girls, "Be

happy. Talk happiness. There is enough sadness in the world without yours." Helen was about to try to end some of that sadness. In her next book, *Out of the Dark*, she finally wrote about something besides herself. It was about solving the problems of the world of 1913: hunger, poor housing, lack of jobs, and cruelty. Few Americans liked this book, for her answers to the problems would mean more taxes for everyone. Helen also wanted women to be able to vote. Few men liked this idea. She wanted the United States to stay out of any wars, although in 1913 a dangerous war was about to begin. It was her first book failure.

There was another failure at home. John had decided that he could not do his own writing while living with Helen and Annie. The Macys' marriage was over. Helen was deeply upset. Annie's health began to fail under the shock. A new young friend from Scotland, Polly Thompson, came to help. She planned to go on vacation with Annie to help her get her strength back. Mrs. Keller stayed with Helen.

Another new secretary, Peter Fagan, was working with them, too. His job was to make sure that all of Helen's letters and writings were finished and sent to the right places. Peter cared very much about Helen, and she came to love him, too. They made plans for a secret wedding. It had to be a secret because Mrs. Keller did not like Peter.

The day that Annie left on vacation, Mrs. Keller learned about the wedding plans. She would stop that! She took Helen home to Alabama and made sure that Peter never saw her again. With all her handicaps, Helen could do nothing on her own, including getting back to Peter. Years later, Helen talked about this sadly, but she said it was probably for the best.

Polly and Annie spent months in warm Puerto Rico in 1916. Helen missed them dreadfully. She missed Peter. She knew John would never work with them again, either.

Mrs. Keller didn't have the time or patience to chat into Helen's hand all day long, as Teacher did. It was a sad time for Helen. When Annie got back, they sold the house that held such unhappy memories for both women. They moved to a new home in Forest Hills in New York City.

"I am paying my own passage through the world and am proud of it," Helen said, but making it on her own wasn't easy. Her books and speeches made some money, but things were tight. In 1919, a movie about Helen's life was begun. Only a few movies had ever been made, and Helen thought it would pay well. She hoped it would cheer other people with special needs to see how much she had done so far. At first, she spent a lot of time helping with the filming. When they started changing around the facts of her life, Helen gave up.

She had wasted a lot of time. Now she really needed money. Instead of movies, people often went to theaters to see live shows. These vaudeville ("VOD-vill") shows were like circuses but with only one act on stage at a time. All sorts of people were in vaudeville: singers and animal trainers, jugglers and magicians, actors and poets. It paid well. Helen and Annie made up an act and appeared in vaudeville shows around the country.

When the curtain opened, Annie, dressed in a beautiful gown, would be sitting at a piano. She told everyone the story of Helen's life. Then Helen, also dressed in satins and lace, would walk across the stage and rest her hand on the piano. She showed how she could tell when the audience was clapping by feeling the shaking of the stage beneath her feet. She smelled the flowers that were always placed in the same spot on the piano. Then she spoke.

Helen explained how, with other people's help, she had learned to talk. "We live by each other and for each other," she would smile. "Alone we can do so little. Together we can do so much." The stage floor always shook after her speech.

Next Annie would spell questions that

people asked into Helen's hand. Sometimes Helen's answers were serious. When asked if she wanted to see more than anything else in the world, she always answered that friendship was more important than sight. She said she would rather walk with a friend in the darkness than walk alone in the light.

Most of her answers were fun. She was often asked if she shut her eyes when she slept. "I don't know," she would answer. "I've never stayed awake long enough to find out!" When asked if she was happy, she answered, "I am . . . because I have books and sunshine and friends and a work that interests me."

The people loved it. They learned more about Helen and about what handicapped people could do. Helen loved it. She was making many new friends, traveling to exciting new places, and earning money, too. The theaters loved having Helen in their shows, for crowds came and paid just to see her.

Annie hated every bit of it. She didn't like

meeting new people or talking in front of the noisy, happy crowds. The lights hurt her weak eyes. She didn't like traveling. And, once again, she wasn't feeling well.

In the fall of 1921, Helen's mother died. Sorrow filled their household.

A few months later, Annie lost her voice and Polly had to take her place with Helen in the act. People were growing tired of vaudeville, and the following year, Helen didn't go on stage. Now there wasn't enough money to feed Helen, Polly, and Annie. There were doctor bills and other payments to make. Helen had to make a decision.

For years, she had made it on her own. Now she needed help. She found it by helping others. The American Foundation for the Blind (AFB) asked her to work for them, raising money for schools that would teach blind people—and others—all that the blind can do. Helen cared just as much about deaf people and their problems, but she knew she was only one person. She could do more good by working for one group of the handicapped at a time. She said yes to the AFB.

"I have set myself with all my mind and all my heart," Helen wrote to a friend, "to the working out and perfecting of a happier life for the sightless everywhere."

# five

The new job brought excitement and happiness to Helen. "Now is the time," she said, "to shake ourselves free from old ideas." Helen hated to be bored. She found change and challenge fun and she loved helping people. Her work with the American Foundation for the Blind was helping to solve problems that made life hard for all blind people.

Braille was the only way that a sightless person could read, but there were at least three different kinds of Braille. Helen, along with all other sightless children, had to learn English and its spelling—plus three different ways to write it! The Braille printers were clumsy, expensive, and easily broken. The foundation spent money to invent new printers and have all books in one Braille language.

As a child, Helen had to travel halfway across the country to go to school at Perkins. The AFB wanted money to help each state start schools for children who were blind or, like Helen, deaf-blind.

Helen had always had trouble finding ways to earn money. That was true of all people with special needs. Half of the problem was that there weren't many jobs that a blind person could do and little job training for blind people. The foundation would set up schools and companies for the blind.

The other half of the problem was how other people thought of the handicapped. They wouldn't hire a person with special needs even if he or she was perfect for the job.

Somehow these people imagined that being blind or deaf or unable to speak meant being stupid, too. The AFB wanted to change this idea, and Helen was just right for the job—*she* certainly wasn't stupid!

Could all these problems be solved? Helen, still an optimist, was sure they could. As a child surrounded by goodness, it had been easy for her to expect things to go well. But now, even after so much sadness and money trouble, Helen was still hoping for the best. And now she could work to make it happen.

Helen gave four speeches a week for the AFB, telling her own story, explaining the problems that all handicapped people face and the ways the AFB was trying to help. Then she would ask the crowd to help, too, by giving money. Even if they didn't give money, they learned how smart and able a blind, deaf person could be.

In the first three years, Helen talked to 250,000 people in 123 American cities. She criss-crossed the country, raising money and showing off her abilities. Though she knew she was helping others, she said that sometimes she felt like a beggar raising money for others. She needed to do something on her own, too.

The company that had published *The Story of My Life* sent a young editor, Nella Braddy Henney, to help Helen start another book about her life. Since John had left, Helen hadn't felt good about her writing. He had helped her choose the best ways to say what she wanted to and had gotten her papers ready to send to the publishing company. Nella would do this, too.

Helen agreed, but she wanted to write something else, first. At 47, she wrote *My Religion* to let people know what gave her the strength to stay joyful throughout her life in darkness. Helen belonged to the New Church. Her church, and the writings of Emanuel Swedenborg, its founder, told her that God had things under control. No matter how it might look at the moment, everything would come out fine. Nothing could shake Helen's faith.

Two years later, in 1929, *Midstream: My Later Life* was published. It covered Helen's life from age 22 to 49. Annie could barely read it.

Teacher was going blind. One eye could not see at all and it hurt so dreadfully that the doctors decided to take it out. Her other eye was sore, too, but it could still see a little bit. The eye operation helped, but, at 64, Annie was stiff and heavy and tired. She stopped going along to speeches with Helen, but traveled to Wales with her in 1930.

The trip was supposed to make Teacher feel better. At first, they all rested. That was good for Annie and Polly, but Helen was never the resting type. She was glad to leave in a few months to tour Ireland and England before coming home.

In 1932, Helen and Annie both were awarded honorary college degrees by Temple University in Philadelphia, Pennsylvania, for the work they had done for the blind. Helen was glad to get the honor. She took it as a "thank you" for all she had done to help others in America. She knew that news of the award, like others she had gotten, would make even more people think about the handicapped.

Annie didn't feel she had earned the honor. She felt that her student's greatness was due to her quick mind, not the way she was taught. Annie had taken Helen through college, but she had never gone herself. All along, she had made sure that the attention went to Helen. Annie refused to go up on stage to get her award.

First one, then another, of the people who filled the great hall rose to their feet. They stood with Helen to show that they felt Annie deserved the honor, too. At last, Teacher and Helen walked up together to be given their degrees.

Helen was very proud of her awards and what she had done in America. But there were blind people everywhere. In some countries, the blind were left to beg in the streets for food. In others, they were put into hospitals for the mentally ill. Many countries had no schools for their blind at all. They needed help.

Helen believed that "the more we try to help each other and make life brighter, the happier we shall be." At 52, Helen had fame and energy. She knew how to make friends—and how to make changes. She was ready to take on the world.

She helped the AFB plan a meeting of people who worked with the blind around the world. Teachers from 32 countries came. They talked about what they were doing and what more they hoped to do for the blind in their own lands.

Helen, Annie, and Polly went traveling again, now to countries in Europe. Annie was tired of traveling and now sick with cancer when they came home. There was more bad news, too. John Macy had died. Though he and Annie had not been together for 28 years, she was heartbroken. The three women went to Scotland to be alone with their sorrow.

That summer in a little town called South Arcan was the last vacation they would take together. Helen taught Annie to read Braille, for now both women were blind. Polly read *Anne Sullivan Macy* aloud to them. It was a new book that their editor, Nella Braddy Henney, had written about Annie. Too soon they had to leave. The world was getting ready for another war and it was time to come home where they would be safe.

Back in Forest Hills, Annie battled with cancer. At age 70, she hadn't much strength left for the fight. On October 20, 1936, she died.

Except for a few months, Annie and Helen had lived together for 50 years. Annie had always chosen what she would tell Helen. That way, she controlled what Helen would "hear" and what she could "see." Annie had always

helped Helen to "speak," too. She had often made lively changes when she told people what Helen was saying. She had looked over and fixed Helen's writing. They had been far more than friends; far more than even mother and daughter. With Annie's death, it seemed a part of Helen had died, too.

# six

LIGHTING THE WORLD

After Annie's funeral, Polly took Helen back to Scotland. Neither of them could bear to stay home with the memories of Teacher's illness and death. Next they traveled to Japan. Months earlier, the Japanese had asked Helen to come and help the blind there as she had in America.

It was a wonderful visit. The Japanese government gave her parties and presents, showed her their schools for the blind and listened to her ideas. Crowds of Japanese children waved sweet-smelling flowers to welcome her. When she said that she had three dogs at home, someone showed her an Akita. Helen ran her hands through the guard dog's soft fur and he gently licked her face. A new Japanese friend promised to send her an Akita of her own when she went home.

Her tour made news around the world for two reasons. In a country where handicaps were thought to be given by God, Helen was showing that those burdens could be lifted. And, though women were not important in Japan, the Japanese were listening to—and caring about—what ladylike Helen had to say.

This was just what she and Polly needed. Here was a reason to go on living after Annie's death. Teacher was gone, but Helen could go on working to help millions of other blind people.

When they came home, the AFB offered to build them a new home in Easton, Connecticut. Helen and Polly named it Arcan Ridge, after the last vacation they had spent with Teacher.

Arcan Ridge was a beautiful house, filled with gifts from Helen's friends. The bookshelves were wide to hold all her Braille books and files. Helen could walk on a pathway by an old stone wall while her dogs ran in the woodlands nearby with the new Akita.

Now Helen was working with President Franklin Delano Roosevelt and the U.S. government to get money for the foundation's programs for the blind. With her help, a law was passed that said all blind people would be given some money to help them support themselves. Another law promised that the government would buy things that were made by blind people's companies. More laws covered schooling and medical care.

Suddenly, World War II came to America. It stunned Helen that her friend, Japan, had attacked first. Helen's travels were over while battles were fought around the world. While

she worked at home, raising money for the AFB, 12,000 other sightless Americans were working to help win the war. Some taught in schools so that teachers with sight could go to battle. Others worked in factories to build ships and bombs. Many worked in hospitals to help the wounded. They were hired because Helen had shown the country that the handicapped could do almost anything.

During the war years, Helen finished *Journal,* a book that she had begun after Annie died. As soon as Helen could write, Teacher had made her keep a journal. Every day she had to write something—a report on the weather, an idea she been thinking about, or perhaps a beautiful poem. Keeping those journals had helped Helen learn to write well and to think clearly. After Annie died, Helen had started a new journal. Writing this one helped her understand her feelings about Teacher's death and the life she still had to live.

Next, she began to write a book about

Annie's life. Helen collected hundreds of their letters to each other and to friends. She made notes in Braille about what she wanted to say and started to write. The book was half done when she took time off in 1943 to tour American hospitals for the AFB.

Thousands of soldiers had been blinded during the war. She visited them and the others who now would have to live with handicaps. It was, she said later, "the crowning experience of my life." Some of the soldiers wanted to talk. Others asked for a kiss, a hug, or just a touch. They felt good that someone so famous cared about them. And they felt braver after seeing what she had done in spite of all of her problems. She even made the busy nurses feel good. One remembered that, in the middle of a long hard day, Helen had felt her face, smiled, and said, "Oh, you are so beautiful!"

Then it was off on more travels to raise money and talk, with Polly's help, about her American Foundation for Overseas Blind.

Though Americans had fought in World War II, there were no battles here. In other countries where battles had been fought, hospitals, homes, and schools for the blind had been destroyed. Many Braille presses were ruined. Helen's help was needed more than ever.

She and Polly traveled around the world for the next ten years. They visited dozens of countries. Everywhere they went, crowds listened to Helen's story and her hopes for blind people. No one who saw her could ever again think that the life of a handicapped person was hopeless.

During a visit to Rome, they heard that their home, Arcan Ridge, had burned down. All of her work on the book about Annie was lost. All of the gifts and Braille books were gone, along with her furniture. Helen had always kept a Bible under her bed. She had read it so many times that the Braille dots were worn right off some of the pages. Her Bible was ashes, too.

The women flew home to the ruins. The stink of burnt wood and fabric was dreadful, but they knew things were much worse in the ruined cities where World War II was fought. The foundation promised to rebuild the house. Friends would give them new furniture. There was nothing more they could do in America, so Polly and Helen went back to traveling.

Between trips, Helen did finally write the book about Annie. She had to use her memory instead of the notes she had lost in the fire. *Teacher,* published in 1955, was the last book Helen would write.

Helen was still busy giving speeches for the AFB and asking for money. Some of the things she did were dull, but she always kept a smile on her face and a twinkle in her eyes, the way Annie had taught her. "People think Teacher has left me," she said, "but she is with me all the time." Helen always looked like she was having a good time with life.

Once she danced with the Martha Graham Dancers. Helen could feel the beat of music through the floorboards. Now she swayed with Martha, the woman who had made a whole new kind of dance, more modern than ballet. As Helen felt the breeze from the slender young dancers whirling about her, she smiled. This time Helen's smile was real.

She liked meeting presidents, kings, and queens on her trips. She enjoyed parties at the homes of many famous people, and invited them to visit her at the new Arcan Ridge. She toured famous parks. Helen's favorite was Niagara Falls. She stood so close that cool spray covered her clothing. She knew just how hard the water crashed and tumbled over the falls by the way the rocks beneath her feet were shaking.

In 1957, *The Miracle Worker*, a play about Annie and Helen, was performed in New York City. It told the wonderful story of how Annie had given Helen her first word, "water," and an

escape out of darkness and anger. It made Helen even more famous than before.

Helen got money from the play, but now she didn't need it. She didn't have to work at all. Old friends had died, leaving their money to her. She and Polly were getting old, too. Helen still had lots of energy, but Polly was cranky and very ill. She did not want anyone else caring for Helen or even touching Helen's hand to "talk" to her. Helen wrote that her religion was helping her to "keep the heart brave and fight out to the end with a smiling face."

Polly's life came to its end in 1960. A year later, Helen had to stop traveling. At 81, a sudden illness had left her feeling "old and tired," and sometimes confused. Now she spent her time at home, reading, thinking, and entertaining friends. A lovely wig, her ready smile, and her pretty blue eyes made her look younger, but Helen was growing weaker year by year.

On June 1, 1968, Helen died at the age of

87. "My life," she said, "has been a wonder-tale of kind people who helped me to light the path of the handicapped." The light Helen lit still shines in the organizations she helped to start, in the countries she visited, and in the mind of everyone who remembers her story.

This book *should* have been easy to write. The facts were everywhere. Helen Keller wrote eight books about herself and what she believed. There are dozens of other biographies of Helen and of Annie. Files bulge with newspaper and magazine articles. People who knew Helen are glad to share what they remember.

But facts weren't enough. I still didn't understand Helen, the person. I am not blind or deaf. How could I write about someone so different from me? Then I read again Helen's plea that we "forget she is deaf and blind and think of her as an ordinary woman."

I had fallen into the same trap that she fought against all her life around the world. I had imagined Helen's mind to be different from mine simply because her senses were.

Handicapped people are just like anyone else—they can be optimistic or gloomy, fun or dull, smart or foolish, powerful or meek. One hundred years after she first started to teach that fact, Helen finally taught me. And *then* I could write this book.

K. V. K.

# TIMELINE / INDEX